Backyard Chickens: The Beginner's Guide to Raising and Caring for Backyard Chickens

by Rashelle Johnson

Disclaimer:

The information contained in this book is for general information purposes only. The statements contained herein have not been evaluated nor approved by the US Food and Drug Administration. This book is sold with the understanding the author and/or publisher is not giving medical advice, nor should the information contained in this book replace medical advice, nor is it intended to diagnose or treat any disease, illness or other medical condition.

While we endeavor to keep the information up to date and correct, we make no representations or warranties of any kind, express or implied, about the completeness, accuracy, reliability, suitability or availability with respect to the book or the information, products, services, or related graphics contained book for any purpose. Any reliance you place on such information is therefore strictly at your own risk.

Dedication:

This book is dedicated to all the backyard chicken keepers and those who aspire to raise backyard chickens. Keep up the good work.

Contents

Why Raise Chickens?

So, you're considering raising chickens? If you aren't 100 percent sold on the idea of raising chickens in your backyard, you probably will be after reading this book. There are a number of reasons why people raise chickens, some of which may be surprising to the uninitiated.

The biggest reason people decide to start raising chickens is to become less reliable on the food sold in grocery stores. Some people are looking to go organic, and they know the best way to ensure they're getting organic chickens and eggs are to raise the chickens and harvest the eggs themselves. Some are survivalists, preparing for a situation in which they have to go off the grid. Others are just looking to save money on their grocery bill.

No matter the reason, raising your own chickens is a rewarding and enjoyable undertaking.

Many people want to begin raising their own chickens, but have no clue where to start. The best way to learn to raise backyard chickens is on-the-job training. Your best bet is to read this book cover to cover, build or buy a coop and a small flock of chickens and get to it. Chickens are inexpensive and easy to raise.

Just don't forget to feed them.

Here are some of the reasons people are raising backyard chickens:

- They want an almost constant supply of fresh eggs.
- They want to harvest fresh free-range meat.

- They want to become less reliant on grocery stores.
- They want to get off the grid.
- To teach their kids basic homesteading.
- They want to harvest the manure for fertilizer.
- Insect and pest control.
- Weed control.
- They make good pets and are fun to raise and watch.
- They want to raise show birds.

Commercial vs. Fresh Eggs

Anyone who's eaten a fresh egg laid by a free range chicken will tell you there's a huge difference in quality between the eggs you get from the store and the eggs you get when you raise your own chickens. Once you've tried a fresh egg, you'll never want to eat another store bought egg again.

They're really that good.

The first thing you'll notice when you crack a fresh egg for the first time is the vibrant color of the yolk and the thickness of the shell. Instead of the pale yellow you're used to, fresh eggs have a vibrant orange yolk. The difference in color can be attributed to a number of factors. For one, the commercial eggs you get from the store have often been laid a week or longer from the date you purchase them. The yolk degrades in quality over time and some of the egg white evaporates as the egg ages.

Another reason for the difference in quality is the diet of the chickens. Commercial chickens are often locked up in small cages their entire lives where they're fed pellets or feed that gives them the nutrients they need to lay eggs, but little more. Free range chickens are allowed to run about as they please, which means they'll be eating a variety of items. Bugs, spiders, grass and weeds are all part of a chicken's natural diet, and their eggs are healthier and better tasting when they get to eat these items.

Yet another factor affecting egg quality is the stress placed on the chicken. Egg farms are often scary places. They have controlled heating, cooling, lighting and feeding systems that place undue stress on the chickens. The cages are usually small, and the chickens are often packed into them so tightly they have trouble moving around. The environment is tailor-made to pump out as many eggs as possible with little regard to the living conditions of the chickens. This all adds up to a stressful environment for the egg layers, which further reduces the quality of the eggs.

Don't fall for the marketing hype of the eggs being sold as "free-range" in the stores. When you think of free-range, you probably think of chickens running about on a farm, scratching and pecking at the dirt. This is rarely the case. Most commercial free-range chickens are kept indoors in large pens that never see the light of day. While the chickens are technically allowed to move around, they're often packed into large pens with thousands of other chickens. These chickens are still being denied the ability to range around outdoors and supplement their diet with the insect and plant matter they need to produce the best eggs.

The quality of the feed given to the farmed chickens is the biggest contributing factor to egg quality. Egg farmers know people want inexpensive eggs, so they may cut corners on feeding costs. This compromises the taste and nutritional value of the egg, but most people don't care as long as they're able to go to the store and buy eggs for less than a couple bucks a dozen.

According to tests run by Mother Earth News in 2007, free-range eggs are nutritionally better for you than store-bought eggs. The testing revealed free-range eggs contain a third of the cholesterol, a fourth of the saturated fat, twice the omega-3 fatty acids, 3 times the vitamin E and 7 times more beta carotene as the eggs you get in the store.

Another test indicated an even bigger difference. A 1988 test run by Artemis Simopolous revealed Greek pastured eggs contained 13 times the omega-3 fatty acids as eggs sold in stores in the US. While there isn't a lot of data available, most of the information that is out there seems to indicate hens raised on pasture produce healthier eggs than those that are not.

Another health concern with conventional eggs is the risk of salmonella. This nasty bacteria can infect the human body, causing cramping, vomiting, diarrhea and fever that can last as long as 72 hours. In extreme cases, a person who contracts salmonella may have to be hospitalized. Death is uncommon, but not completely unheard of.

While eggs from chickens raised on free ranges in clean coops aren't completely devoid of salmonella, the risk of contracting it is thought to be much lower. One British study found salmonella to be much more prevalent in larger commercial farms than it is in organic or free-range flocks. 6.5 percent of the free-range farms and 4.4 percent of the organic farms tested positive for salmonella. A whopping 23 percent of the farms with hens that were caged tested positive.

What You Need to Raise Chickens: You Might Be Surprised

You aren't going to need much by way of supplies to raise chickens. They're one of the least expensive farm animals to raise.

This makes them a great starter animal for the backyard farmer because it's so easy to start raising them. All you have to do is gather a handful of supplies and buy your flock. This chapter assumes you're buying chickens that are grown and are ready to lay eggs. We'll cover hatching and incubation in a later chapter.

The Coop

If you've decided to raise chickens, the first item you're going to need is a place to house your flock.

A chicken coop is a small building where female chickens are kept. If you're raising chickens because you want to harvest eggs, you're going to want your coop to have nesting boxes. These are dividers into which your chickens can sit and lay eggs. It's also a good idea to include perches the birds can use when it's time to sleep.

There are two broad schools of thought when it comes to coops. The first states that chickens are tough critters that prefer fresh air to being confined in an enclosed coop. Coops built by these people have a lot of open spaces and are well-ventilated. They have roofs to protect the chickens from the elements, but don't do much to insulate them from the cold. They're often little more than a frame with wire mesh stretched across it to keep the chickens in that's covered by a roof to keep rain, sleet and snow off of the chickens. You'd think this sort of coop would only be viable in temperate climates, but they're in use all over the world.

The other school of thought states that chickens are better off in a more controlled environment where they aren't as exposed to the elements. The coops built by these folks are the traditional coops you think of when you picture a chicken coop. They're similar to small buildings and provide an extra layer of protection between your chickens and the environment. They also provide more protection from the prying eyes of predators.

I'm of the opinion that the second type of coop works best, especially in cooler environments. Chickens seem to do best when they have somewhere to get out of the weather and avoid drafts. A good coop will be well-ventilated, but will be able to be closed off when the weather takes a turn for the worse. Chickens can handle cold weather, but they handle it best when their coop is protected to the point where cold drafts aren't blowing through it. Adding windows allows you to open the coop up during warmer months and close it off during the cooler months.

You can either buy your own supplies and build a coop yourself or you can purchase a kit that comes with everything you need, along with instructions on how to put it together. If you're the handy type, it'll cost you a lot less to buy the supplies you need and build your own from scratch. They really aren't all that hard to build.

You can find a bunch of tutorials on how to build coops of all shapes and sizes at the following website:

http://www.backyardchickens.com/atype/2/Coops

Buying a coop kit will cost you anywhere from a couple hundred dollars all the way into the thousands of dollars, depending on the size of the kit you buy and the features you want it to have. This is the way to go if you don't know a Phillips head from a flat head and want the path of least resistance.

You can get good coop kits from the following online stores:

http://www.chickensaloon.com/

http://www.greengardenchicken.com

http://www.chickencoopsource.com/

http://www.chickencoopmart.com

http://www.mypetchicken.com/catalog/Chicken-Coops-c3.aspx

http://www.williams-sonoma.com/shop/agrarian-garden/agrarian-garden-chicken-coops/

I'm not affiliated with these stores in any way, shape or form. I'm providing these links to make things as easy on you as possible. There are a number of other stores where you can buy coop kits.

You can also buy pre-built coops from Craigslist or your local feed supply store. This is a good option is you don't feel like doing any assembly work and just want to get started raising chickens.

Coop Design

When it comes to coop design, the possibilities are endless. You can build a simple coop with just the basic necessities, or you can get fancy and build one that has automatic doors, windows and cleaning systems. It all depends on how handy you are and how easy you want to make things on yourself later on down the road.

Most people like to start off small and expand their flock once they've learned the ropes.

Don't make the mistake of building a coop that's only capable of handling a small group of birds. When you decide you want to grow your flock, you'll have to build or buy a new coop. It's much easier to build a bigger coop than you need the first time around. That way you can expand as you see fit.

There are a handful of basic rules you should follow when it comes to coop design.

The following rules of thumb will help you keep your flock of chickens happy and healthy and maximize the amount of eggs produced:

- **The inside of your coop needs to be easily accessible, so you can get inside and clean it.** A locking door or access panel will make your life easier while keeping predators at bay.
- **Use screws instead of nails.** Screws won't back out the same way nails will.
- **You're going to want one nesting box for every 3 to 5 hens you have.**
- **You need 4 to 5 square feet of space per bird.**
- **Adding a roost will keep your birds happy.** There should be 6" to 10" of roost space per bird. The roost should be at least 2" in diameter and have rounded edges.
- **Floors should be slightly angled toward the door to make your coop easy to hose out and prevent pooling of water.**
- **The coop should be predator- and pest-proof.**
- **Adding an electric light for every 25 to 30 square feet of space will ensure your chickens lay eggs year-round and will keep them warm during the colder months.**
- **Keep feeders and waterers off the ground.** If you leave them at ground height, your chickens are going to make a mess by scratching and rooting in them. Place them high enough so your chickens can reach them with their heads, but can't get into them to scratch around.
- **Your coop should be well-ventilated, but not drafty.** Add windows that can be opened and closed when the need arises. Windows should be

covered with wire mesh to prevent predators from getting in.

Chicken Tractors

Figure 2: Chicken tractor.
By wisemandarine (Mon tracteur à poules, avec les poules) [CC-BY-SA-2.0 (http://creativecommons.org/licenses/by-sa/2.0)], via Wikimedia Commons

A chicken tractor, also known as a chicken ark, is a mobile coop that can be moved around to different places in your yard. It allows you to reap the benefits of letting your chickens roam free, while keeping them safe from most predators. They're a good option for areas where there are too many predators to completely free range chickens, but you don't want to keep your birds cooped up in a single area.

You can place the tractor in an area for a couple days until the chickens have picked it clean of bugs and grass, and then move it somewhere else so they'll have a fresh area to pick the next day.

You can buy (or build) chicken tractors in a wide variety of sizes. Small ones can be picked up and moved by hand, while some of the larger ones come with wheels and a tow hitch, so you can hook a tractor up to them to move them around. If you want free-range birds that are kept relatively safe, a chicken tractor may be your best bet.

Nesting Boxes

Figure 3: Nesting boxes. By Jessica Reeder. Photo by Margie Burks. (IMG_0529) [CC-BY-SA-2.0 (http://creativecommons.org/licenses/by-sa/2.0)], via Wikimedia Commons

If you want to harvest eggs from your chickens, you're going to want to include nesting boxes in your coop design. Hens prefer a dry, dark place they can go to lay their eggs. If you provide this for them, you'll get better eggs and more of them.

You're going to want one nesting box for every 3 to 5 hens you have. A good nesting box will be at least 14" wide by 14" deep and will have adequate room for your hens to stand up in. This usually means building boxes with at least a foot of headspace.

Nesting boxes should be raised off the ground by at least a couple feet. Your chickens will jump up into them to lay their eggs. Keep the nesting boxes below the height of the roosts or your chickens might roost in the boxes instead. If you still have trouble with your chickens roosting in your nesting boxes, try blocking them off at night. After a couple weeks, the chickens will get used to using their roosts and will no longer use the nesting boxes.

You don't want your chickens roosting on top of the nesting box and making a mess of it. The best way to prevent this from happening is to build a box with a sloped roof. A slope of 45 degrees will prevent your chickens from hopping up there and lying down at night.

Your chickens are going to want comfortable nesting material on which to lay their eggs. Traditionally, straw has been used as bedding material. This isn't the best choice because it tends to be damp and holds moisture. This can cause problems with mold and mildew, especially in humid environments. That said, a lot of people use straw or hay to good results. It's an economical choice that won't break your budget and the chickens seem to like it because it's easy for them to mold around.

Corn cob or dry wood shavings are a good choice for nesting material. These are easier to clean and don't hold moisture like stray and hay does.

One thing's for certain. No matter what nesting material you use, your chickens are going to kick it all over the place. There's no reason to use expensive bedding material when it's going to end up spread all over the coop.

Roosts

A roost is a place you provide for your chickens to sit on when they want to sleep. Most chickens will seek out the highest point in the coop when it's time to roost, so you want your roost to be higher than everything else. If your nesting boxes are at the same level as your roost or above it, your chickens may end up roosting in them instead.

Ideally your roosts will be at least 2 1/2 feet above the ground and no more than 4. Place them too high off the ground and older chickens will have trouble jumping up to them. Too low and your chickens will look for other places to roost.

You want your roost to be at least two inches across and to have edges for the chickens to grab onto. You should provide enough roosting space so all of your chickens will be able to roost at night. Most breeds need 6" to 8" of roosting space per chicken.

Wood is the most common material used to build roosts. I've seen people use 2x4's, 2x2's, tree branches and even pallets with a couple of the slats removed as roosts. 2x2's work best for smaller chicken breeds, while the 2x4's are good for the bigger, heavier breeds of chicken. If you use tree branches, be aware the cracks and crevices in the branches can provide hiding spots for mites. Treating your roosts with NEEM can prevent mites from living in them.

P a g e | 22

Make sure your roost is properly supported. Depending on the breed, a single hen can weigh between 2 and 10 pounds. If you have 10 chickens, your roost may need to be able to support as much as a hundred pounds.

Chickens poop a lot at night, so don't place the roosts above nesting boxes, food or water. A "poop board" can make your life a lot easier when it's time to clean the coop. This is a board that's placed beneath the roost onto which the chickens poop. If you use a poop board, build one with a lip and fill it with sand. All you'll have to do to clean it is use something to sift the poop out of the sand.

If your chickens are climbing onto the poop board and scratching around in the sand, a hanging poop board may be necessary. Hang the board from the roof with wires or chains, so it swings around when the chickens try to hop onto it. They don't seem to like this and it usually stops them from jumping up on the board.

Ventilation

Chickens produce a lot of moisture and their feces contains ammonia, which can fill a poorly ventilated coop with fumes. A properly ventilated coop will have enough holes in it to allow dampness, heat, fumes and humidity to escape before it has a chance to build up and cause problems.

A poorly ventilated chicken coop can become a damp, dingy place in a hurry. Chickens breathe out water vapor much in the same way humans do. It might surprise you to find out chickens don't pee. Instead, they get rid of extra moisture in their poop. Chickens are largely immune to the cold if they're in a ventilated coop that's dry. Put a chicken in a moist, damp coop in the cold and you open the chicken up to all sorts of health problems, not the least of which is frostbite.

While you might assume you don't want your coop to be well-ventilated in a cold climate, it's these climates in which ventilation is especially important. Damp conditions in extreme cold temperatures can lead to frostbite and increased chance of illness.

Leaving chicken poop to sit in a poorly ventilated coop can do respiratory damage as the ammonia level in the air increases. You might argue that you clean your coop regularly, but chickens poop a lot and their coops are always going to have some level of ammonia fumes in them. Letting these fumes sit can cause respiratory problems in your chickens and will make them more susceptible to illness and disease.

A properly ventilated coop will have a number of ventilation slots and holes in it through which air can move naturally. Warm air rises, so adding vents at the top of your coop can help keep air constantly circulating through your coop, especially during the hot summer months.

If you don't think vent holes are going to provide enough ventilation, you can add electric fans and turbines to help move air through your coop. While electric methods can help in times of need, they shouldn't be your sole ventilation method. If the fan or electric air pump you're using fails, you don't want all of the humid ammonia-fill air to be stuck in your coop until it's fixed.

Be sure to cover your vent holes with wire mesh or some other type of covering that will keep predators out. You want air to be able to move through your coop, not predators that get in through the vents.

The number of vent holes you're going to need depends on the climate you're living in and how many chickens you're planning on keeping in your coop. Plan for at least one vent hole per chicken you're going to have in the coop, more if you're in an especially humid area. Don't go too small on the size of your holes. You want them to be at least 1' x 1'. In areas where it gets hot in the summer, you're going to want even bigger holes. Double or triple the size of the holes to get enough air moving through your coop.

When you cut your vent holes, you're going to want to figure out a way to securely close them off when you don't need them. A hinged panel that can be caulked shut will keep drafts out during cold weather. During extreme weather or when it's especially cold, you can close off the vents you don't need to keep the weather out and provide a more comfortable environment for your birds. When it's cold outside, the only vents you want to have open are the ones at the top of your coop. These vents will keep the air in the coop fresh and prevent moisture from building up, but won't create a cold draft through the coop that will make your chickens uncomfortable.

Feeders and Waterers

There are countless ways you can feed and water your chickens. Some work much better than others. It helps to keep in mind that chickens are messy creatures that love to get into their food and water and scratch around. If you have open trays of food, your chickens will quickly scratch all of the food out of the trays and into the coop. They'll still eat it, but it can create quite a mess—and it'll attract rodents and other creature looking for a quick meal.

Homemade Feeder Tutorial

You can make your own feeder out of a bucket and a metal or plastic pan with a couple inch lip. Here are the step-by-step instructions on how to make a bucket feeder:

1. Get a drill with a large paddle bit and drill multiple holes along the bottom edge of the bucket.
2. Glue or bolt the pan to the bucket so that any food that falls from the holes you drilled will fall into the pan.
3. Hang the bucket in your chicken coop so it's high enough that the chickens can only reach into the oil pan by craning their necks a bit.
4. Remove the lid from the bucket and add chicken feed to it. Some of the feed should fall out of the holes you drilled along the bottom edge of the bucket into the pan.
5. Replace the lid.

While you can buy fancy feeders that do pretty much the same thing, this feeder will get the job done for less than ten bucks.

If you want to use a bucket feeder on the ground, find a pan into which the bucket fits and leaves maybe an inch or two space between the bucket and the edge of the pan. Anymore and your chickens are going to scratch feed out of the pan onto the ground.

Homemade Waterer Tutorial

You can create a watering bucket using the same supplies you used to make the feeder. You're going to need a bucket with an airtight lid. Here are the instructions:

1. Drill small holes close to the bottom edge of the bucket. These holes should be slightly lower than the top of the pan. The water will seep out of these holes and will fill the pan with water until the holes are covered. If the holes are above the lip of the pan, the water will overflow over the edges of pan and spill into your coop. Leave enough space between the top of the pan and where you drill your holes so your chickens won't spill water into the coop every time they get a drink.
2. Glue the bucket down. It should be securely attached to the pan before you add water to the bucket.
3. Remove the lid and fill the bucket with water.
4. If you made it correctly, the bucket will leak water into the pan until the holes are covered. As the

chickens drink the water, more water will seep from the holes in the bucket.

This waterer doesn't work well when it's hung. If you want to get it off the ground, create a platform on which to set it.

Treadle Feeder

Your feeder may attract wild birds and other animals looking to capitalize on the free meal being left out every day. A treadle feeder will allow you to feed your chickens without having to worry about other lightweight animals and birds getting to the feed.

The treadle feeder has a lever attached to a platform onto which your chickens have to jump in order to open the feeder. There's a cover over the feed that raises when a chicken steps up on the platform. When the chicken steps off the platform, the lever is released and the cover falls back down over the feed.

You can purchase a metal treadle feeder online for around $200. Here's a link to a nice one for sale from GrandpasFeeders.com:

http://www.grandpasfeeders.com/products/standard-chicken-feeder

If you're feeling industrious, you can build your own. Woodworkingcorner.com has plans you can use to build your own wooden treadle for a fraction of the price of the commercial one above. Here's a link to the plans:

http://www.woodworkingcorner.com/feeder.php

Here's a tip not included in those plans. If you build a treadle feeder and find your chickens aren't heavy enough to open the cover, don't scrap your treadle. All you have to do is add counterweights to the platform your chicken jumps on to make it heavy enough so your lightest chicken jumping on the platform will activate it.

Chicken Nipples Make Watering a Breeze

For a cleaner approach to watering where you can place the bucket wherever you'd like, chicken nipples can be a lifesaver. Chicken nipple jokes aside, these handy little items can be inserted into PVC piping and each nipple provides a spot at which your chickens can drink. You can also drill holes into the bottom of a bucket and attach the nipples through the holes to create a gravity watering system.

You can run the PVC piping from the bottom of the bucket and can get as creative as you want with where you set up your chicken's watering space. Just be sure to seal all corners and joints with silicon or PVS glue to avoid any leaks. You don't want water leaking into your coop.

If you want to buy chicken nipples, you can get them from your local feed supply store or from Amazon.com. They'll run you about $10 for six nipples and will make your watering tasks a breeze.

Chickens

Well, of course. You're going to need chickens in order to raise chickens. That makes total sense. We'll cover the various breeds of chickens in a later chapter.

The number of chickens you get is entirely up to you. It's a little easier to start small and work your way up to larger numbers of chickens, but these are pretty tough birds. They're rather forgiving and won't die off quickly if you make a mistake—unless it's a huge one.

Bedding (Litter)

Chicken coop bedding, also known as litter, is material you lay down on the floor of the coop to help knock down moisture and to absorb water spills. It helps keep the coop clean and smelling fresher than it would if you didn't have the bedding. You're going to want at least four inches of bedding on the floor of your coop.

Good bedding material is absorbent, cheap and safe for your chickens. It's insulates the ground and prevents it from getting to warm or too cool.

The following items are commonly used for bedding:

- Straw.
- Sand.
- Wood shavings.

Let's take a closer look at each of the types of bedding.

Wood Shavings

Wood shavings are the best material to use as bedding, but buying enough to cover a coop floor can get expensive in a hurry. Shavings are absorbent and suck up excess moisture. The chickens like shavings because they can stir them up and give themselves a dust bath.

Check with your local sawmills or with the city to see if they offer shavings for cheap. Sawmills will often offer shavings (or sawdust) for a low price, as long as you're willing to load it into bags yourself. The city may create shavings when they cut down trees. They often offer these shavings up for sale to the public for low prices.

Pine shavings are the best wood shavings to use. Steer clear of cedar shavings because they contain oils that can irritate your chicken's lungs.

Sand

While some people use fine sand like that found at the beach or the playground, I've found the coarser and grittier the sand works better as chicken litter. You can get gritty sand by the truckload at your local gravel yard. It's cheap, too. You can get it for less than $10 a ton. That's right, I said ton. 50 bucks will buy you enough sand to last a long, long time.

It not only works well as litter, it provides grit for your chickens, so it saves you from having to buy that. Chickens will swallow some of the small pebbles and gravel to help their stomachs digest food. This is a good thing, as you might otherwise have to add grit to your feed.

Sand is hands down the easiest material to clean poop out of. All you have to do is scoop the poop out of the sand once every couple of days and you're good to go. No worries about scooping up sand with the poop. The cost of sand eases all worries of having to replace it. If you plan on adding the poop to your compost heap, use a kitty litter scoop to sift the poop out.

You only have to change your sand once or twice a year, and that's only if you feel it needs to be changed. I change it out when it starts to look dirty and dingy, but that's just because I like my coop to look and smell clean.

One warning about working with sand. Over time, it can be ground down into a fine dust that fills the air and can make you sick if you inhale enough of it. Wearing a mask while working with the sand in your coop is a good idea.

Straw

Straw has been in use as bedding for hundreds of years. It's inexpensive and easy to source. Chickens like it because they're able to scratch around in it and certain types of straw have grains of the plants that the straw was made from in them, so the chickens will scratch around in it looking for a tasty snack.

The downside to using straw is it tends to hold moisture and isn't ideal for humid conditions. You want to keep your bedding as dry as possible, so if you're using straw and you notice it's starting to get damp and clump up, you're going to need to add more dry straw. You can also throw a few handfuls of feed into the straw. The chickens will scratch around in it, which will help break it up, allowing it to dry out faster.

The Deep Litter System

You can cut down on the money you're spending on shavings by implementing what's called a deep litter system. With this system, instead of cleaning your coop out once or twice a week, you only do it once every three to six months. Instead of cleaning your coop once a week, go in and mix up the litter. You can throw feed in the bottom of the coop and let your chickens do this for you when they scratch around to get to the feed. Add a thin layer of new shavings to the coop each week.

By the end of the three to six month period, you'll have a thick layer of shavings mixed with poop in the bottom of the coop that can be harvested and added to your compost bin. Scrape it out, wash your coop down and do it all over again. This method doesn't work very well if you have a wood floor for your coop. It can cause the wood to rot.

You'd think this method would cause your coop to stink so bad you wouldn't want to enter it. If it's done right, there is no smell. I was amazed the first time I saw this done, because I couldn't believe there was no smell. Try it and see for yourself. The key is to continuously vent the ammonia from the coop and to keep turning the litter so it dries all the way through.

Free-Range Chickens

Free-range chickens are allowed to come and go as they please. They scratch around your yard or property looking for tasty snacks and return to their coop in the evening. You'll still have to feed and water your chickens, just not as much as you'd have to if they were constantly cooped up.

Go to the egg section at any grocery store and you'll notice the free-range eggs command a premium price over the regular eggs. The reason for this is they cost a little more to produce, but people are willing to pay more for them because they're healthier and more nutritious. This is because free-range chickens are allowed to roam around freely and supplement their diets with bugs, plant matter and anything else they're able to scratch up.

Happy and healthy chickens lay healthier and tastier eggs. It's a little more work, but it can be well worth it to let your chickens run around and eat what they want for at least part of the day.

The problem with keeping free-range chickens lies in keeping them safe from predators and other threats like vehicles and people. One of my neighbors has a rather large flock of free-range birds and I constantly see them getting hit by cars while roaming around near the street. I can't help but wonder how many birds a year he loses to cars alone.

Keeping predators away from your free-range birds can be a problem. You're sure to lose a few birds here and there to roving predators, but there are a handful of things you can do to keep them safe. You can train your dog(s) to protect your birds, but it's going to take a lot of work to teach them not to attack your birds, let alone to protect them. It can be done, but it isn't easy. More birds are lost to dogs than are saved by them and it can be frustrating to walk into your yard and see your dog with a bird in his mouth, especially when the dog was supposed to be protecting them.

You're going to want to provide a roosting and nesting area for your birds to keep them from falling victim to nighttime predators. It's a good idea to still have a coop or an area you can lock up at night to keep your birds safe. When you buy new birds or move young birds outside, you're going to want to keep them locked up in the coop for a few days straight. This will teach them the coop is home and they won't stray too far from it. They'll return to it every night when it's time to bed down.

An option that isn't quite free-range, but comes close (while providing more protection for your chickens) is to keep your birds in a chicken tractor that you move around daily or even throughout the day. Your birds stay safe and still get to root around in different areas of your house and yard on their hunt for food to supplement their diet. You can also set up portable fencing that keeps your birds in a certain area on your property. To further deter predators, you can set up electric fencing around your portable pen.

Some people "yard" their birds. They clip their wings to keep them from being able to hop over the fences in their yard and let them run free in the yard during the day. If you use this technique of letting your birds run free, be aware that any predator that manages to get into your yard will be able to easily catch chickens that aren't able to fly to nearby roosts to get away.

Another tip to help keep your birds safe is to choose breeds of chicken that are dark in color and blend in with the natural surroundings. A white bird really stands out when walking through a field and makes it much easier for a predator to home in on it and attack.

Having a rooster or two around can also help protect your flock. Roosters are constantly scanning for danger and will let the hens know when they spot it. Hens aren't as capable at spotting danger as roosters are, and they're more prone to falling victim to predators when there isn't a rooster around. The problem is roosters tend to get rather noisy in the morning and it can cause problems with your neighbors if you add a rooster or two to the mix, especially in areas where you aren't supposed to keep chickens.

Remember that your chickens are going to need a readily available source of food and water. If there's a natural pond or river nearby, that'll work for the water. If not, you're going to have to provide water for your birds. As far as food goes, your chickens may need you to provide at least some feed, especially during the cold winter months where plants and insects are scarce.

Instead of providing food and water in one location for your chickens, try to spread it out across their natural range and switch up the locations where you place the food. This will help keep them instinctually hunting for food and will prevent them from getting lazy and automatically going to the place they know food will be found. This will also help prevent predators from setting up shop by a known food source and dining on your chickens when they come to eat.

Supervised Free-Ranging

If you live in an area where there are a lot of predators or other threats to your chickens, you may want to do supervised free-ranging. This entails letting your chickens out to free-range, but only while you're around to watch them do their thing. This allows you to keep a watchful eye out for predators, while ensuring your birds get to free-range for at least part of the day.

The best time to do supervised free-ranging is during the evening hours as the sun starts to fall. During these hours, predators are often just waking up or are preparing to bed down and they usually aren't actively hunting. Your birds are less likely to fall prey to hungry predators during this time, especially if you're watching them.

Dawn is another good time to do supervised free-ranging, but dusk is better because your chickens will return to their coop as night starts to fall. If you let your chickens out in the morning, you're going to have to try to round them up and get them into their coop when you're done supervising. Anyone who's tried that can attest to how difficult it is to herd chickens. It's much easier to let them free-range in the evening when they'll return naturally to their home coop.

Stay close to your chickens and they'll begin to see you as the leader of the flock. You can even learn to roll your tongue in a low cluck to alert them of danger. If done right, they'll all head back to the coop when they hear you cluck.

At the end of the free-range period, do a head count of your birds as they return to the coop. Seek out any stragglers and lead them back to the coop with a few treats.

Be careful not to leave any chickens out overnight or you're probably going to lose them.

Breed Selection: How to Select the Right Breed of Chicken

There are a lot of difficult decisions that have to be made when you start raising chickens. One of the most important decisions you're going to have to make is what breed of bird you want to raise. Pick the right breed and you're going to be happy and have a constant source of food. Choose the wrong breed and you'll have is problems.

There are four basic categories of chickens:

- Meat chicken.
- Layer chickens (egg birds).
- Combination birds.
- Show birds (not covered in this book).

If this was all you had to choose from, selection would be easy. All you'd have to do is choose whether you want meat, eggs or both and you'd be good to go. It isn't that simple. There are a wide variety of breeds that fall into each of these categories, so once you've picked a category, you still have a lot of narrowing down to do.

Meat Chickens

There are a couple basic types of meat chickens.
Broiler chickens are birds that are raised to be eventually killed and eaten. They aren't so much a specific breed, as they are a combination of breeds that have been bred to promote quick growth. Broiler chickens are typically harvested when they reach the 4 pound mark, which usually happens right around the time they hit two months of age. Roaster chickens are kept until they grow to between 5 and 10 pounds, which usually happens when they're between 3 to 5 months of age.

Cornish rock chickens are the most common type of broiler. They're bred to grow to 4 pounds in 6 to 8 weeks, at which time they should be harvested. If you want to breed chickens solely for meat purposes while using the least amount of feed per bird, these are the birds you want to raise.

You can buy Cornish rock chicks for less than a buck a piece. If you buy a bunch of them, you can get them for closer to $0.50 each. They can't be bred to good result, so you're stuck buying chicks every year. Another problem with CX chickens is they don't willingly free range. As long as you have feed present, your birds are going to eat the feed instead of ranging about looking for food.

Free-range broilers will cost you a little more per chick, but are a much better option if you want your meat birds to be free range.
These birds don't mature as fast as the Cornish rock chickens. It takes 9 to 10 weeks for them to reach a weight

of 4 pounds. The meat you get from these chickens tends to be leaner because they roam around looking for food.

If you're looking to raise chickens that look and taste good, you might want to go with free-range broilers. They come in a number of shapes and sizes, as opposed to the Cornish rock chickens, which are boring white birds. The free range broilers are fun to raise and watch. Just don't get too attached to them. You're raising them for meat, not to be kept as pets.

Cornish game hens are birds that are raised to be butchered at a younger age. They reach maturity at around a month to a month and a half and are butchered when they are around 2 pounds.

These tasty young birds are typically served as a single serving. A family of four would normally consume four Cornish game hens in a single meal.

Most meat chickens are cross-bred birds that can't be raised to maturity and bred to get the same type of chicken as the parent. You never know what you're going to get when you breed meat birds. You're much better off just buying the chicks. If you want to breed your meat birds, find a Heritage breed or go with dual purpose birds that have been bred to both be harvested for meat and to lay eggs.

Laying Chickens

Laying chickens are bred for the purpose of laying eggs. The best type to buy depends on whether you want to eat the eggs or to hatch them into chicks. Hens that will sit on eggs and hatch and raise chicks are said to go broody.

The following breeds of chicken are great egg layers if you want to harvest eggs for food:

- **Delaware.** These white and black birds will lay brown eggs at the rate of an egg a day when they mature. You can eat the males when they mature.
- **Leghorns.** These chickens produce white eggs and the best layers are capable of upwards of 250 eggs a year.
- **Mille Fleur Bantams.** I've heard mixed reports on this breed of chicken. Some people say they are good layers, but from my experience, the eggs tend to be a bit on the small side.
- **New Hampshire Reds.** These large birds are capable of laying an egg a day. They lay brown eggs and are a good choice if you want to raise free-range chickens.
- **Rhode Island Reds and Whites.** These chickens lay great tasting brown eggs. Hens can lay as often as once a day.
- **Sex-link birds.** There are also a number of hybrid birds, known as sexlink birds, that are crosses of various breeds. Sex-link birds have been bred for a number of purposes. Check with

the breeder to see the individual traits of sex-link birds you're interested in.

- **Spangled Hamburgs.** Great layers and beautiful birds. They produce a lot of eggs, but can be a bit skittish. They will fly away if given the chance.

The following breeds of chicken are great at hatching their own eggs into chicks:

- **Rhode Island Reds and Whites.** Rhode Island birds are good at hatching their own eggs as well. These birds are great if you're looking for a sustainable source of eggs because you can hatch and raise your own chicks to create more laying hens.
- **Plymouth Rock:** The hens will go broody. The males are good to eat. These birds can be raised to create a sustainable food source.
- **Silkies.** Broody Silkie hens have such a strong maternal instinct they can be used to hatch eggs from other breeds of chickens. They generally aren't eaten and their eggs aren't of the best quality.

Dual-Purpose Chickens

Dual-purpose chickens are decent layers and are able to be eaten. These birds are a good choice for those who want both eggs and meat:

- **Rhode Island Reds** were mentioned in the previous chapter because they're great laying chickens. They're also pretty good to eat, which makes them a good dual-purpose bird.
- **Ameraucana chickens** are also good dual-purpose birds. This breed is fun to own because the hens lay eggs that are blue. Araucana chickens lay eggs that are blue, green and pink, but they're harder to raise from chicks because a lot of them will die before hatching.
- **New Hampshire Reds**, also mentioned in the laying section, are decent dual-purpose birds. They tend to be a bit on the aggressive side, so you need to take care to acclimate them to new birds you add to your flock.
- **Sussex chickens** are also great dual-purpose breeds. They can be found in a number of colors and are both good layers and are good to eat.

You'll see a number of chickens being sold by breeders that are listed as dual-purpose. There are quite a few Heritage breeds available, which are naturally mating breeds that have withstood the test of time. There are also hybrids available, which are crosses of other breeds.

Feeding Your Chickens

Looking for the easiest way to feed your chickens? Simply purchase a complete feed from your local feed supply store. It'll have everything your chickens need to stay healthy.

You're still going to have to pay attention to what you're buying because complete feeds exist for various ages and types of birds. Chicks and growing birds require different nutrients than full-grown birds and aging birds. There are different feeds for birds you plan on using as egg layers and birds you want to cook and eat. It's rarely a good idea to buy all-purpose feed and feed it to all of your chickens, especially if you have different ages and types of chickens in your coop.

You can supplement your complete feed with a number of items to ensure your chickens are happy and healthy. Whole grain can be tossed out onto the ground in your coop to get your chickens to scratch around and turn over the litter. You can also add pasture or lawn clippings to your bird's diet. If you do this, try to use fresh clippings from young plants. The older a plant is, the harder it is for a chicken to digest.

Calcium should be made available to your chickens. It may seem strange, but egg shells can be saved, dried and given to your chickens as part of their diet. It's important that you clean and dry the shells prior to feeding them to your chickens. You can also use crushed oyster shells to add calcium to your chicken's diet.

From time to time you may want to give your chickens a treat. The following treats are safe to give to your birds occasionally, but shouldn't be a staple in their diet:

- Apples.
- Applesauce.
- Bananas.
- Blackberries.
- Bread.
- Broccoli.
- Cauliflower.
- Cheese.
- Cooked chicken meat. That's right, chickens are cannibals.
- Cooked eggs.
- Cooked fish.
- Corn.
- Green beans.
- Insects.
- Leafy greens.
- Oatmeal.
- Peaches.
- Pears.
- Popcorn (plain)
- Raspberries.
- Seeds.
- Shredded carrots.
- Squash.
- Strawberries.
- Table scraps.

- Watermelon.
- Whole grain.

When it comes to feeding, it's best to feed your birds in a manner called "free-choice." What this means is there's always food available. When your birds are hungry, they can go and get it. When they're done eating, they'll stop. Chickens aren't known for continuously gorging themselves on food just because it's there.

Stuff You Shouldn't Feed Your Chickens

Chickens are tough birds that can eat most of the stuff we eat. Like humans, there are also a number of items your chickens shouldn't eat. I'd steer clear of feeding them any plant matter that you aren't sure about, because there are quite a few plants that can harm your chickens.

Here's a list of some of the plants you shouldn't feed your chickens:

- Apple seed.
- Apricots.
- Artichokes.
- Balsam apple.
- Balsam pear.
- Belladonna.
- Bishop's weed.
- Buckwheat.
- Cactus.
- Cherries.
- Chives.
- Clovers.
- Daffodil.
- Elderberry.
- Flax.
- Foxtails.
- Garlic.
- Holly.
- Horse chestnut.
- Hyacinth.

- Ivy.
- Jasmine.
- Kale.
- Leeks.
- Lima beans.
- Marijuana. It'll get your chickens high. Yes, seriously.
- Milkweed.
- Mistletoe.
- Mushrooms.
- Mustard.
- Oak.
- Oleander.
- Onions.
- Oranges.
- Parsnip.
- Peaches.
- Plums.
- Poison ivy and oak.
- Poppy.
- Potatoes.
- Rhubarb.
- Sage.
- Soybeans.
- Sugar beet.
- Sunflower.
- Tobacco.
- Tomatoes.

Keep in mind that this is only a partial list, and just because an item isn't on the list, you shouldn't automatically assume it's OK. Your best bet is to steer clear of anything you aren't sure of.

Diatomaceous Earth

The first time I heard of diatomaceous earth, I thought it was a special kind of dirt. It isn't. It's actually made up of the broken up shells of tiny creatures that lived en masse millions of years ago. These shells are harvested and sold by the bag to people like you and me. Diatomaceous earth works by slicing into the hard exterior shells of insects and killing them. It's perfectly safe for humans to consume, just be careful breathing this fine powder in. Too much of it can cause respiratory issues.

There are a couple uses for diatomaceous earth in regards to chickens. The first involves adding it to your chicken's dust bath area to keep mites and bugs down. You can also spread it around the coop, but that can get rather expensive.

I included this section on diatomaceous earth in the food section because you can also add it to your chicken's feed. It'll kill off internal parasites and worms and is approved by the FDA as a feed additive. Add it to your chicken feed at 1% to 2% for best results.

Predator Control

Here's a sampling of the predators you may need to keep away from your chickens:

- Alligators and crocodiles.
- Badgers.
- Bears.
- Birds of prey.
- Bobcats.
- Cats.
- Coyotes.
- Dogs.
- Foxes.
- Lizards.
- Mink.
- Mountain lions.
- Opossums.
- Raccoons.
- Rats.
- Reptiles.
- Skunks.
- Weasels.
- Wolverines.
- Wolves.

In order to protect your hens, it helps to know what you need to protect them from. Larger predators are going to be more persistent and can push right through barriers that would keep smaller predators at bay. Don't underestimate the ability of a predator to get at an easy chicken dinner. Many a chicken has been lost while housed in a coop the owner thought was secure. It's better to overdo it when it comes to protecting your chickens. Nobody has ever complained about having a coop that's too secure.

Alligators and Crocodiles

Alligators and crocodiles will both make short work of a chicken that happens to stumble into their path. If you live in an area where alligators and crocodiles are prevalent, you're going to want to take steps to keep your chickens away from open water sources where these predators may reside.

Free-range chickens are most likely to fall victim to alligators and crocs. They walk up to a body of water and get snapped up by a hungry gator. In order to prevent this from happening, you have to keep them away from areas where alligators reside.

If you keep your chickens in a coop and they aren't allowed to run free, you're relatively safe from alligators and crocodiles. They're ambush hunters who hide by the shoreline and attack anything that happens to walk by. Keeping your chickens away from the shore is key to keeping them out of the mouths (and stomachs) of hungry gators.

If you're worried about gator wandering onto land and happening upon your chickens, a 5-foot chain-link fence near the water source should keep them at bay. Gators and crocs can't climb tall fences, so a fence of this height is enough to hold them off.

To be completely honest with you, alligators and crocodiles are rarely a concern when it comes to chickens. While they will snack on a chicken that's an easy meal, you probably won't lose many chickens to gators, even if you live in an area where they hang out.

Large Predators

It's tough to stop larger predators like bears, mountain lions, wolves and coyotes because they can often push their way right into even the sturdiest of coops. And once they get in, they do major damage to your flock. A single bear can wipe out every bird you own in one fell swoop.

Before we get into things you can do to get rid of large predators, let's first cover something you shouldn't do. You should not attempt to go out to your coop to shoo the large predator away. This is a good way to end up dead, especially if the predator is in a killing frenzy and is attacking your birds. Your chickens are not worth your life.

If it's legal to shoot the animal attacking your crops, you can do so if you please.

At times, that's the only way to get rid of an animal that's found your coop. They'll keep coming back until there isn't an easy meal there for them anymore or you take steps to permanently get rid of them. If you do decide to shoot a large predator, make sure you know what you're doing and are using a powerful enough rifle to take them down from a distance. You don't want a wounded and angry animal attacking you, especially not one big enough to do serious damage.

I've heard stories of people using frozen paintballs to scare large predators away, but don't recommend this practice because you'll have to get close to them to shoot them and they may turn on you if the paint balls make them mad or scared enough.

Want a less lethal method of keeping bears and large predators out?

Electric fences are your only other real option. You're going to want a fence charged with 5,000 to 6,000 volts to deter bears and other large animals. If you're interested in more information on electric fencing, here's a link to a great document put out by the Virginia Department of Game and Inland Fisheries that explains how to set one up:

http://www.dgif.virginia.gov/wildlife/bear/fencing.pdf

Mid-Size Predators

Mid-size predators like cats, raccoons, badgers, mink, skunks and possums can really wreak havoc on your chickens if they're able to get to the coop. It isn't unheard of for these predators to get into a coop and kill everything in it. Raccoons have even been known to reach through holes in the coop and kill chickens before pulling them out of the coop a piece at a time.

You want to take every reasonable step you can to fortify your coop against these predators. They will do whatever they have to do to get at an easy meal. They'll try to dig under, climb over and have even been known to use brute force to push their way into a coop. Some predators are smart enough to open simple locks and latches. A good way to test the security of your coop is to ask a 6-year old kid to try to get in. If a kid can easily bypass the locks or push their way in, most predators will be able to get in as well.

You're going to want to build a coop strong enough to withstand an attack from one of these predators. Use strong wood that's screwed together in multiple places. If you're able to shake your coop apart, a mid-sized predator will make short work of it. Don't leave any gaps in the wood or any open windows into which they can sneak at night.

The roof of the coop needs to be secure. A plywood roof that's securely screwed to the frame is probably your best bet.

Predators may try to dig under a coop to get at the chickens inside. If you've done any research into building a coop, you may have seen people recommend digging wire into the ground to keep predators from digging under the coop.

This method works, but don't underestimate the ability of a predator to dig its way in. Your best bet is to attach fencing securely to the bottom of the coop and set it 2" to 4" below the surface. It should extend out at least 16" in any direction from the coop. Predators will tear through the lighter gauge stuff, so you should use heavier gauge wire. Chain link fencing works well. Galvanized hardware cloth is another good choice that's hard for predators to get through.

Once a predator has found your chickens, it'll keep coming back until you take steps to eliminate it or keep it away from your birds. If it's legal, shooting the predator may be your best bet.

If that isn't an option, you can put up an electric fence around the outside of your coop. Try staggering two strands of electrified wire a foot apart. Place one a foot off the ground and the other right on the ground at the base of the coop, so anything that attempts to burrow in will get shocked. They should be close enough together so a predator that makes it past one wire will land on the other.

The same type of electric fence that protects against large predators will work for small predators as well.

The mid-size predator that poses the largest threat to your chickens isn't a wild animal at all. It's dogs that are the biggest threat—namely yours and your neighbor's domesticated pets.

Some dogs are great around chickens and will protect them from other predators. Others, not so much. Bird dogs and dogs with a strong hunting instinct will attack chickens and quickly kill them.

A single dog can tear up a large number of birds in a short period of time if it isn't stopped. It's a good idea to talk to your neighbors when you start raising your chickens and let them know your expectations regarding their dogs. They should be told that you'll expect them to pay for any birds their dogs come into your yard and kill. Agreeing on how an attack on your birds will be handled before an attack happens can help things go smoothly later on down the road if one does take place.

Fencing off your coop may be your best option to keep the peace with the neighbors. Be sure to make the fence tall enough that roaming dogs can't jump into it or cover the top. If a dog is able to jump into a fenced off area with chickens inside, you've just made killing your birds a heck of a lot easier.

If it's your dogs that are the problem, you can probably train them to stay away from the chickens.

There are no guarantees when it comes to dogs and chickens, but with enough work, you can keep your birds relatively safe from your dogs. I know there are people who don't like to use shock collars, but they can be a valuable tool in training your dog(s) to stay away from the chicken coop. Place the collar on them and let them outside a few times a day when you're training them. When they get close to the coop, yell "NO" loudly and give them a zap. They'll get the message quickly and learn to stay away from the coop.

It's also possible to train them without use of a shock collar. You can lead them out to the coop daily on a leash and walk them around by the chickens. Any attempt to play with or attack the chickens should be cut short by a hard jerk on the leash and a loud "NO!" This sort of training will teach your dogs there is a negative reaction associated with "playing" with the chickens. It'll take some time, but your dogs should eventually get the point.

Small Predators

Small predators like rats, ferrets and weasels are cunning critters that may try to sneak into your hen house, where they'll either try to eat your eggs, your chickens, or both. They've been known to chew, dig and sneak their way into chicken coops.

The same things that work for mid-size predators also work for small predators, but you have to pay close attention to detail. Small predators can squeeze through tiny gaps. You're going to need to go over your coop with a fine-tooth comb to ensure there are no gaps smaller predators can get into.

An adult rat can squeeze through a hole a little larger than a quarter. Young rats can squeeze through even smaller holes. When rats are a concern, hardware cloth works better than wire because it doesn't have holes in it that the rats can get through.

While rats probably aren't going to prey on full-grown chickens, they will dine on chicks and eggs. Gather all of your eggs in the evening, so there's nothing left for rats to dine on. Chicks should also be gathered and secured in a small cage that rats can't get into. Rats can be trapped or poisoned. Just be careful not to leave the poison or the traps where your chickens can get to them. You're also going to have to keep a close eye on your coop because chickens will eat dead rats. If a poisoned rat dies in your coop, you need to get it out of there as soon as possible.

You're going to have to work hard to keep small predators out of your chicken coop. They're persistent little buggers that will stop at nothing to get in. They've been known to chew their way through small-gauge wire like chicken wire and wood. You're going to have to constantly monitor your coop for signs of predators chewing at it. They'll work at it over a long period time until they eventually work their way in. The best way to prevent this from happening is to keep a close eye on your coop and repair any chewing damage as soon as it occurs. If you notice damage, set up a trap or two nearby. You might be able to catch the critter the next time it comes around.

Sometimes small predators get into your coop no matter what you try. Even when you bury wire to keep them out, they may be persistent enough to burrow their way in. When they breach your defenses, the best thing to do is go on the offensive. Traps baited with peanut butter are irresistible to rats and mice, but you need to place them so your chickens can't get to them. Build a wooden box with a small hole in it large enough for the rats and mice to get in, but too small for chickens to get into. Set the traps at the back of the box, so your chickens aren't able to stick their heads in the hole to reach them.

Here's a tip I wish I would have known about when I was just getting started raising chickens. Small predators have been known to nibble on the feet of chickens while they're roosting. This can lead to all sorts of complications later on down the road.

If you're having this problem, use 2x4's for your roosts and set them so the 4" side is facing up. Your chicken's bodies will cover their feet when they roost on the 2x4's, which will solve this issue.

Birds of Prey

You don't just have to worry about keeping your chickens safe from attacks on the ground; you also have to worry about birds of prey swooping in for an easy meal. Hawks, eagles and owls will all dine on chickens if they can swoop down on them from above.

In areas where birds of prey are abundant, you can lose a lot of chickens to these predators—and you can't lay a finger on them in defense. They're protected under the Migratory Bird Treaty Act. You can get in big trouble for harming a bird of prey, even if you catch it attacking your chickens and try to fight it off. In fact, getting caught with a single feather in your possession can get you in a lot of trouble, and doing harm to one of these birds can land you in jail.

The best way to keep your chickens safe from birds of prey is to prevent them from swooping down on them from above. Birds of prey sit up high or fly in circles looking for food. When they see a tasty meal (like a plump chicken), they dive down at it from above and hit it, often killing on contact. After the kill, they take their victim to a safe area to eat it.

Chickens in a coop with a covered top are relatively safe from birds of prey. If the bird of prey can't see your chickens or get to them from above, they're pretty much safe.

It's a little more difficult to protect chickens that are allowed to roam free. One way to help your free-range birds survive is to provide areas where they can hide when they see the tell-tale shadow of a bird of prey overhead.

This won't completely eliminate kills from birds of prey, but it can help cut down on death from above.

Another method is to string fishing line back and forth across areas your chickens are allowed to roam in. The bird of prey won't swoop down on your chickens out of fear of getting caught in the fishing line. Just make sure not to leave big enough gaps in the line that a bird of prey can get through it.

Reptiles

Reptiles, namely snakes, will kill and eat chickens if they think they're able to swallow them. A good-sized snake can swallow many breeds of chicken whole, while smaller snakes will go after hatchlings and eggs. Don't be fooled into thinking you only have to worry about snakes if you have chicks or juvenile chickens. The bigger snakes have been known to kill full-grown chickens.

A lot of people recommend killing any snakes found around the chicken coop, but you may cause other problems by doing this. Snakes aren't always a bad thing to have around because they kill and eat other small animals like rats and mice. If you kill off the indigent snake population in your yard, you might touch off an explosion in the population of rodents.

A better bet would be to take steps to keep snakes from getting into your coop. Wire mesh works well to keep them out. It's going to take some effort to ensure your coop doesn't have any snake-sized holes in it, but it's worth the effort. I've also heard of people spreading sulfur around the outside of the coop to deter them. They say it burns the snakes belly as it tries to slither over it. In order for this method to be effective, you have to spread it in a complete circle surrounding your coop.

Brooding Chicks

In order to brood chicks, you're going to need fertile eggs. You can buy fertile eggs or you can keep a rooster or two around to fertilize the eggs your chickens lay.

Eggs you plan on hatching need to be incubated within a week of the time they're laid for best results.

Your incubator needs to have a constant temperature between 99 and 102 degrees F. There shouldn't be any fluctuation in the temperature and it should never be allowed to go outside of this range. Your best bet is to get an incubator with a thermostat to ensure the temperature is kept in the correct range. Otherwise, you'll never know if the temperature fluctuates when you aren't around.

When you first add eggs to your incubator, the temperature will drop a bit. This is because the cool eggs bring the ambient temperature in the incubator down. This is normal and the temperature will go back up as the eggs warm up. Don't adjust your temperature setting or you run the risk of overheating your eggs once the temperature in the incubator normalizes.

In addition to temperatures between 99F and 102F, your eggs need the humidity in the incubator to be around 53%, give or take a couple percentage points. Most incubators have a water tray that sits below the egg holders. Add warm water to this tray to bring up the humidity. If not, you can add a wet sponge to the incubator to up the humidity.

Chickens take approximately 21 days to hatch. Turn the eggs 3 to 4 times a day for the first 18 days. Stop turning them three days before they're supposed to hatch. Increase the humidity to 63% to 65% the last three days. Once your chicks hatch, drop the temperature in the incubator to 95F for a couple days until the chicks have dried.

Don't be surprised when all of your eggs don't hatch. If you have a 70% to 85% egg hatch rate, you're doing well. If none of your chicks hatch, or they hatch, but have problems, you need to examine your incubation process. The eggs either weren't fertilized correctly or they weren't kept at the right temperature and turned correctly.

Raising Chicks

Chicks are fairly easy to care for. All you need to do is make sure they're warm and well-fed and watered. You've also got to protect them from predators.

If you're keeping your chicks indoors where they're safe from predators, you can keep them in a cardboard box.

Place two to three inches of wood shavings or sand in the box. Lay down a sheet or two of paper in the box for the first couple days, so the chicks don't eat the litter. You can remove the paper once they've been eating feed for a couple days.

Keep them warm using a light bulb. The temperature inside the box should be around 95F to start. As the chicks mature, you can adjust the temperature down. Monitor your chicks to see whether the temperature is too hot or cold for them and adjust it as necessary. Cold chicks will huddle together and shiver. Chicks that are too warm will have their mouth open and will be panting. You can change the temperature inside the box by bringing the lamp closer to the box or moving it further away.

You need a waterer that's designed to keep the chicks out of the water. They'll get into it and will get chilled if you don't keep them out. A small dish with pebbles in it will keep the chicks out of the water while allowing them to drink when they want.

Start your chicks off on starter feed. This feed will allow them to grow at a rapid pace. Keep a constant supply of feed at the ready for your chicks. They'll eat a lot as they grow and you don't want to stunt their growth because they don't have enough food available.

Chicks are easy to raise as long as you keep them fed, watered and warm. Keeping them safe is easy if you raise them indoors. If you raise them outdoors, you're going to need something more secure than a cardboard box.

Build a wood box that'll keep predators at bay. Make sure it's strong enough to keep larger predators like cats and dogs out. Make sure you don't have any gaps into which smaller predators can squeeze. There aren't too many predators that won't make a quick meal out of a chick. It's up to you to make sure they're safe.

Getting Hens to Lay and Sit on Eggs

The amount of daylight a hen is exposed to is the number one most important factor that determines whether or not she'll lay eggs and sit on them.

Hens are programmed to lay eggs and sit on them in the spring, when daylight hours are in the range of 15 to 17 hours a day. During the spring, hens are naturally inclined to lay eggs and go broody.

You can add lighting to your coop to ensure your hens lay eggs and want to sit on them during the rest of the year. Set your lights on timers to ensure your hens get 17 hours of light every day of the year. This will trick their biological clocks into thinking it's springtime the entire year.

Broody hens will lay a clutch of eggs and they'll sit on them until they hatch. Some hens are more inclined to going broody than others. If your hens go broody, you can leave the eggs in the coop and the hen will hatch them into chicks. If your hens won't go broody, you're going to have to incubate the eggs yourself.

There are a few things you can do to improve the chances of your hen going broody. The amount of light the hen is exposed to should remain at 17 hours a day and shouldn't fluctuate. Provide the hen with a comfortable nesting box filled with straw that she can move around as she sees fit. The nesting box should be dark and should provide the hen with privacy.

Fertilization of Eggs

Which came first? The chicken or the egg?

My response to this question is it had to be the rooster. You have to have a rooster to mate with your hens or you won't get any chickens. The rooster will hold the hen down by the back of her neck during the mating process. You're going to want 1 rooster for every ten or so hens to ensure all of your hens get the semen they need to lay fertilized eggs.

A fertilized hen will lay fertile eggs for up to a week after mating. Hens will still lay eggs when there is not rooster present; the eggs just won't be able to be hatched into chicks. The egg will be an edible egg, but no matter how long you try to incubate it, it'll never develop into a chick.

You can't really tell whether an egg is fertile or not until it's had a chance to develop. You can candle your eggs after a few days to see if they're developing. The candling process involves holding the eggs up to a light source in a dark room to see whether they're starting to develop. A bloody area with tendrils snaking away from it will be visible in fertile eggs that are starting to grow. Eggs that don't show this embryo or that have a bloody ring instead of the embryo should be discarded because they haven't been properly fertilized.

Monitor the progress of your eggs as they continue to develop. You should be able to see the embryo develop into a chick. It's an amazing process when it works right, and you'll soon learn to distinguish healthy, developing eggs from those that don't develop properly.

Chicken Laws & Ordinances

I apologize in advance for the bad pun, but you don't want to run a-fowl of local laws and ordinances. Cities and counties have ordinances and laws regarding backyard chickens. It would take a book 10 times the size of this one to list all of the rules and regulations—and it would be outdated by the time it was published.

Instead of attempting to cover all of the laws regarding raising chickens here in this book, I'm going to tell you that you need to contact your local government offices to find out exactly what the laws are that you have to follow.

Just so you aren't surprised, here are some of the items that are regulated by various laws and ordinances:

- Noise made by your chickens, especially the crowing of roosters.
- Distances chickens must be kept from roads and other residences.
- The breeding of chickens.
- The number of hens and roosters you can keep.
- The size of your coop.
- How many birds are allowed per square foot in your coop.
- Whether or not you're allowed to let your birds free-range, even if they're kept on your own property.
- Some areas require that permits are purchased raise chickens or build coops.

- Keeping chickens is banned altogether in some areas.
- There may be restrictions on selling chickens and/or eggs without a permit.

You might be surprised to find out you live in an area where keeping chickens is forbidden by law. While I would never recommend breaking the law, I will tell you this. People are keeping chickens in areas where it's not allowed, and they're doing so successfully and without much fanfare.

This is usually done by keeping the neighbors happy. An agreement under which eggs are provided to neighbors in order to keep them quiet is working for thousands of people across the nation. The problem with trying to hide chickens lies in the fact that you probably aren't going to be able to keep your birds a secret forever. Your neighbors may get tired of your birds or get mad at you for another reason and rat you out. Or they might move and the new people who move in aren't as understanding of your flock.

Your best option is to fight back against unfair ordinances. You more than likely aren't the only person in your city that wants to raise chickens. Gather a group of like-minded individuals and take the issue to the city council. You might be surprised to find they cave in when they see how many people want to raise chickens. They don't want to get voted out of office and will usually cave to popular pressure.

The End of the Book, the Beginning of Your Journey

I hope you enjoyed this book and that it provided you with the information (and the desire) to start keeping your own backyard chickens. If you liked the book, a positive review would really help me out.

If you have any questions or comments, I can be reached at the following e-mail address:

mike_rashelle@yahoo.com

Feel free to contact me any time you'd like.

Printed in the USA
CPSIA information can be obtained
at www.ICGtesting.com
LVHW022338071123
763357LV00032B/816